Freedom of Dependency

by

Patricia Mussolum

Mill Lake Books

Mill Lake Books
Abbotsford, BC, Canada
https://jamescoggins.wordpress.com/mill-lake-books/

Cover illustration: Watercolor by Patricia Mussolum
Cover design by Dean Tjepkema

ISBN: 978-1-7771926-1-7

Table of Contents

Introduction

The idea of a relationship with the Creator of the universe seemed preposterous to my human imagination. On the other hand, there is an unexplainable hunger in human beings to connect with something greater than ourselves. Maybe it's just to make ourselves greater in our own eyes, to be set apart, to be different. Or maybe it is the realization that there really is more to life than just eating, sleeping, and physical comfort.

I came to realize that it was God Himself who had initiated that hunger in me to feel unique, valued, and loved—and to see myself as created by Him and connected to Him. After all, I didn't create myself. I breathe the air He created, and I remain on earth's surface due to the gravity He produced. I'm living now, as opposed to living earlier or later in history, because of His choice. I have explored other religions, and I have (rather reluctantly at first) examined Christianity. When I did so, I discovered that in Jesus Christ God was offering, not just another religion, but a relationship. He was inviting me to accept Him as Love itself. Philosophy, eastern religion, atheism, science, and meditation just didn't cut it. Neither did success. Having a husband, a career, two beautiful children (one of each), and a brand

6

new home weren't enough to satisfy me.

A significant event for me occurred on the way to church one Sunday in July. I wasn't expecting much, as I was just performing what I saw as my religious duty. But we passed a barn that had a piece of scripture displayed on its side, declaring "Jesus Christ the same yesterday, today and forever" (Hebrews 13:8). I didn't understand then that God means it when He declares that his Word does not return to him empty but will accomplish the purpose for which He sent it (Isaiah 55:11). That piece of Scripture on the side of the barn did not fail to have its intended effect. God was already using it to turn my focus to Jesus.

I sat in the balcony of that country church, and very privately (without my family knowing), and rather hesitatingly and with some fear, I asked Jesus to come into my life. That seemingly ordinary Sunday set the course of my life. I couldn't suppress the tears. I had no words to tell my family what I had just done. But there was sudden relief and an inner freedom I had never experienced before. It was as if a light had come on. The colors of nature were magnified, and my path was changed forever.

It was all so astoundingly simple. That was when I began to learn that God's love is demonstrated in the person of Jesus. This was the unfathomable solution to my search. There is no Plan B. It's God's Son Jesus or nothing. We have only one earthly father, and likewise we have only one heavenly Father. Jesus says that He Himself is the way, the truth, and the life and that no one comes to the Father except through Him (John 14:6).

As with any offering of love, the one making the offer runs the risk of rejection. Jesus has been, and continues to be, rejected by many to this day. But true love doesn't cease at the door of rejection. God's love is unending and undeterred. He takes the chance.

Jesus wants us to call God "Father" because He is our Father.

Jesus has called us His "friends" because we are.

Chapter 1

The Sorting Room

Once I had entered into a relationship with God through Jesus, there was much to sort out. I needed God to clarify what this new relationship looked like. I meditated on scripture, and as I did, God brought clarity into my confusion. "If anyone is in Christ, he is a new creature," I

11

read. "The old things passed away; behold, new things have come" (2 Corinthians 5:17). Jesus said that we must be "born again" (John 3:3). This terminology has caused confusion for many, but I knew something miraculous had happened to me. I realized that I really had been born again spiritually. I was seeing the evidence.

For the first 30 years of my life, I followed the normal, expected course—get an education, get married, have kids, buy a house, and live happily ever after. The only thing missing was satisfaction. Money, good health, a career, marriage, two kids, and a new home just didn't cut it. I asked Jesus into my life because every other way to fill the inner void had failed. I chose the God who described Himself as "Love," the God who asked to have a relationship with me and wanted to be my Father. No other religion offered a God who loved me enough to die for me.

There were still many things I had to learn. I understood that Jesus had died for sinners, but I didn't see myself in that category. I had been taught that I could expect God to communicate with those who trusted Him, so I began talking to God. I asked Him what sin I had committed that He had had to die for. After all, in my cocky attitude, I thought I might be the exception!

God did answer me. He said, "You have committed the worst sin of all. It's called pride. You have put yourself and your 'goodness' on a pedestal. You have compared yourself with others in judgment." My eyes were opened to see the truth. I had, in fact, placed myself on a pedestal. I understood that I would have been among the accusers of the woman

13

caught in adultery (John 8:1-11), among those who condemned others for the sins they themselves were guilty of.

God opened my eyes to see how precious His children were—He declared that He loved them so much that He gave Himself up for them (John 3:16, Galatians 2:20, Ephesians 5:25). God also gently taught me that He was not condemning me but rescuing me from myself...and so the need for the new birth. God enlightened me to accept that he saw His Son in me.

It took me many years of trudging through stacks of sermons and teachings before I realized the enormity of being "born again." What a perfect way to describe the experience! To be born is to be conceived. Every child carries the DNA of his or her parents. Until I received Jesus, I only had the DNA of my earthly parents. Now I have a Father who has counted every hair on my head (Matthew 10:30) and knows my every thought (1 Chronicles 28:9). My mom and dad certainly didn't know those details.

Over and over, I was taught that I still had the old sin nature. But how could that be the case if I had been born again? I have come to realize that there is no partial birth. Unfortunately, I had been taught that when I was tempted, it proved that I still had the sin nature. However, Jesus was tempted as well, and He didn't have a sin nature. Hadn't I received His divine nature when I had been born again? I struggled for years with confusion, and then one day I decided to just accept what Jesus had died for. The book of Romans teaches that I am to consider myself "to be dead to sin, but alive to God in Christ Jesus" (Romans 6:11). So, if I'm to consider myself dead to sin, then why should I be entertaining the idea that I have a sin nature?

Other thoughts tormented me: "Who do you think you are? Isn't that a rather prideful attitude? God gives grace to the humble, you know." Before giving my life to Jesus, I had read a book entitled *Satan Is Alive and Well on Planet Earth.* It became very obvious to me that there is darkness in this world. One of Satan's weapons is to accuse us of our weaknesses and to have us question our new identity. Studying Jesus' life, I came to realize He didn't downplay His relationship with his Father or His own identity. Before He began His earthly ministry, He spent some God-ordained time in the desert (Matthew 4:1-11). I personally believe it was to settle once and for all His power over the temptations of the spiritual enemy of humanity. One of the first temptations He experienced during His desert trial was the slimy question, "If you are the son of God..." The same question surfaces when we see ourselves as failures and weak in some areas. It's from the one who accuses and condemns. It sounds like this: "You say you don't have the sin nature, but you just did..." Our confident answer should be: "Therefore there is now no condemnation for those who are in Christ Jesus" (Romans 8:1) and "It is God who is at work in [me], both to will and to work for His good pleasure" (Philippians 2:13). We are also reminded that the God "who began a good work in [us] will perfect it until the day of Christ Jesus" (Philippians 1:6).

The book of Galatians states that God is pleased to reveal his Son in us (Galatians 1:16). Do we see His Son within us? When Jesus died on the cross and gasped out, "It is finished" (John 19:30), He meant it. That is why the apostle Paul could confidently write, "I have been crucified with Christ; and it is no longer I who live, but Christ lives in me" (Galatians 2:20) and "He rescued us from the domain of darkness and transferred us to the kingdom of His beloved Son" (Colossians 1:13).

Paul also wrote: "Test yourselves to see if you are in the faith; examine yourselves! Or do you not recognize this about yourselves, that Christ Jesus is in you—unless indeed you fail the test" (2 Corinthians 13:5). If we are in Jesus, we have been born again, we are a new creation, we have been adopted as God's children, we have become part of the Kingdom of God. That is very reassuring. If we take a hard look at ourselves and realize we are not yet born again, then Jesus' offer is still open. He is inviting us to be made alive.

Chapter 2

Friendship or Formality

After I accepted Jesus, scripture suddenly came to life. God began to reveal truth to me, and I began to share what He taught me. God communicates with us through His Word, the Bible. Dreams and visions and circumstances and incidents in our lives also contribute, but most important is His Word.

How frequently we've stated that we've "changed our minds" regarding a direction or decision. Science is now proving this ability to be vitally true. Nowhere is this more true than in making decisions about ultimate reality. God's Word is full of life, and we can choose to believe it…or not. But how can we know if it is true and full of life? Well, how do we know how an apple tastes unless we bite into it? Food might look delicious, but until we actually taste it, it's just an observation and we can't know for sure. The same is true for God's Word. Only when we read it and decide to trust it will we know that it is true and that it gives us life. Consider the air we breathe and the gravity that holds us here. We may not understand completely how they work, and we often take them for granted, but they are God's laws for life, and we have learned that we can trust them. We will find the same is true when we decide to trust the Bible.

Reading God's Word for ourselves will become a personal experience, not a secondhand passing on of information. It will transform our thinking and therefore our lives. God invites us to "be transformed by the renewing of your mind" (Romans 12:2) and to "taste and see that the Lord is good" (Psalm 34:8).

Although our relationship with God cannot be reduced to a formula, beginning the day with Him is wise. We should remember that we are connecting with Love Himself and that our Father wants to share our life. His plans are always for our best. Psalm 5:3 says, "In the morning I will order my prayer to You and eagerly watch." Prayer is just talking and listening to God…right now, present tense. There may be decisions to make, courses to follow, concerns on our heart and mind. He will guide us through. Sometimes we just toss our prayers up to Him without another thought. However, we are reminded in this verse to "eagerly watch." That would mean watching and listening, staying engaged, expecting a response. There are a million ways He might respond. An email. Another person's offhand comment. A change in our plans. An interruption. An encouraging thought. God's answers are often very personal and unexplainable. Most often, and most dependable, is an answer given through God's Word itself.

For example, one morning I found myself with a big day ahead of me that I couldn't change because my plans involved a number of other people. I was feeling very weak due to a virus. I asked God what to do. The scripture surfaced in my mind: "Let the weak say I am strong" (Joel 3:10 KJV). I wondered why God seemed to be telling me to ignore my symptoms. But God says His ways are not mine (Isaiah 55:8), so I decided to do just that. I could talk, so I said out loud repeatedly (when no one was listening), "I am strong!" In a matter of a few short minutes, I really did feel strong, and the day full of activities went smoothly. Who knew? Well, God knew, of course.

Paying attention when God brings a passage of scripture to our minds is vital. Sometimes God's guidance will mean changing our plans or resting when we were planning to be active. He is always present tense, and there is no time when He is not loving us.

I remember one morning after a few busy days when I was beating myself up for lack of motivation. I asked Him what His thoughts were. His answer was: "Resting is something to do. Stop striving. There is no room for guilt." I had always chastised myself for being lazy if I was not accomplishing something. But Jesus asks us to come to Him when we are weary (Matthew 11:28). He gave us the example of going away by Himself (Mark 1:35). So, one day He told me to say I was strong, and another day He told me to rest. Both directions were perfect.

We can rely on His Word when He says: "His compassions never fail. They are new every morning" (Lamentations 3:22-23). When we learn to listen, He promises: "I will instruct you and teach you in the way which you should go; I will counsel you with My eye upon you" (Psalm 32:8).

Psalm 42:8 says, "The Lord will command His lovingkindness in the daytime," and in Isaiah 45:2 God promises, "I will go before you and make the rough places smooth." Well then, shouldn't we expect things to actually go smoothly if we trust Him? Trusting is something that happens when we know someone has our best interests at heart. We know we can trust a good earthly father and a dependable friend. How much more can we trust our loving heavenly Father! Well, what about when Jesus told us that in this world we would have tribulation (John 16:33)? The next part of the verse says to "take courage." Why? Because Jesus says, "I have overcome the world." God reminds us that "My thoughts are not your thoughts. Nor are My ways your ways" (Isaiah 55:8).

God also invites us to ask Him about our concerns: "Call to Me and I will answer you, and I will tell you great and mighty things, which you do not know" (Jeremiah 33:3). I remember how astounded I was when I first discovered this promise. God was inviting me to call on Him and at the same time promising that He would answer me. This was the God of the universe!

Of course, this would mean that we actually need His wisdom and guidance and that He gives it. But to receive His wisdom, we must actually talk to Him about it. We also need to recognize that *how* He answers will most likely be different from what we imagine, but we can still be assured that it will be for our good and His loving purposes. In response to these truths, we may say: "It is good to give thanks to the Lord and to sing praises to Your name, O Most High; to declare Your lovingkindness in the morning and Your faithfulness by night" (Psalm 92:1-2).

Chapter 3

Getting Dressed

Genesis 3 relates the story of how Adam and Eve, when they became aware that they had disobeyed God, covered themselves with fig leaves. People today often do something similar.

But if we have been born again through Jesus, we no longer have to hide behind fig leaves of any kind, for we are not the same persons we used to be. Sin no longer is master over us. We have a new nature. That is what Jesus meant when He stated that we must be born again. He said He came to set us free (Luke 4:18, John 8:32-36)…free from ourselves! It takes a while for our minds to absorb this truth, and it takes a good dose of courage to trust God. But when Jesus declared on the cross, "It is finished!" (John 19:30), He meant it.

We must then be careful that we don't clothe ourselves with filthy rags. Isaiah 64:6 describes those acts by which we attempt to please God as "a filthy garment." Instead of filthy rags, we should accept God's offer to clothe us in the righteousness of Jesus Christ. When we do this, our hearts become quiet and peaceful, and we can sense His love without trying to earn it.

Think for a moment of parents whose relationship with their children is based on how well the children perform each day and what the children have done to please the parent. That is not how God sees us. The Father sees His Son in us. We are related to Him. He clothes us with His robe of righteousness (2 Corinthians 5:1-4, Ephesians 4:24, Revelation 7:13-14). It's His doing. From God's point of view, it's the only, and the most important, clothing we have.

In the past, I have been deceived into putting on the filthy rags of "works." In my early days with Jesus, I watched other Christians involved in various activities and tried to copy them. The only Christians worth much in my way of thinking were missionaries, pastors, and evangelists. I see this attitude continue to play out in the lives of young people today. Excited in their walk with God, they follow the encouragement of other people to go on mission trips. This is all well and good if God has actually led them to undertake those trips. Often, though, their experiences end in a dismal return to real life and a feeling of disappointment that their efforts were fruitless. No wonder. Instead, it would have been more fruitful for them to learn to hear God's voice for themselves and then follow Him. Basking in God's fatherly love for them would show them that following Him is not a formula pushed on them from outside but an inside personal experience with the Spirit. Young believers need to learn how to listen to God's voice. They should not make the mistake I made of focusing on what other Christians were telling me instead of listening to Jesus within.

Jesus used the illustration of Him being a Shepherd and us being His sheep. It is obviously silly for the sheep to run ahead in an attempt to please the Shepherd and at the end of the day to congratulate themselves on the great acts of service they have done for Him.

Jesus said, "I am the good shepherd" (John 10:11) and described what it means to be a good shepherd: "The sheep hear his voice, and he calls his own sheep by name and leads them out…he goes ahead of them, and the sheep follow him because they know his voice" (John 10:3-4). Note that the sheep follow the Shepherd, not lead Him. The well-known twenty-third Psalm further describes how the relationship with the shepherd works. We must have our minds renewed in order to enter into the experience of dependency. After all, we are following the direction of the King of the universe. He loves us, and we need to let Him call the shots. Then we can relax and rest in the green pastures He leads us to. He knows our thoughts (1 Chronicles 28:9) and has counted and collected every tear we've ever shed (Psalm 56:8). No one else knows us that personally.

The robe of righteousness is armor against the enemy (Ephesians 6:14) and a light around us (Romans 13:12). It is Christ himself. It's beautiful, and it's royal. We should be sure to put it on every day. Colossians 3:12 describes what this robe looks like: "compassion, kindness, humility, gentleness, and patience."

Looked at another way, we should be careful not to wear the yoke of slavery. It doesn't come from God.

Chapter 4

The Vine

In John 15:5, Jesus told His followers: "I am the vine, you are the branches." Branches receive. They don't supply the vine with life, and they can't survive without being connected to the vine. Jesus said in John 10:10 that He came so that we should have life, abundant life. He also stated that He could do nothing Himself without the connection to the

Father (John 5:19,30). Similarly, He said that we can't do anything without being connected to Him (John 15:5). We, like Jesus, must embrace the source! If we believe in Him, we share His life as surely as branches share the life of the vine.

In John 8:12, Jesus said, "I am the light of the world." And then He added: "He who follows Me will not walk in the darkness, but will have the Light of life." In Matthew 5:14-16, Jesus said to His followers, "You are the light of the world...Let your light shine before men in such a way that they may see your good works, and glorify your Father who is in heaven." He warns us against hiding His presence under a bushel basket.

Jesus is described as the cornerstone of the church (Matthew 21:42, Ephesians 2:20). We also are described as "living stones...being built up as a spiritual house" (1 Peter 2:5).

Jesus described Himself to the woman at the well as the source of living water (John 4:10). Jesus also said this of anyone who believes in Him: "From his innermost being will flow rivers of living water" (John 7:38). God promised in Isaiah 58:11: "You will be like a watered garden, and like a spring of water whose waters do not fail." We are most satisfied when we give to those who are thirsty or hungry, either in the physical realm or the spiritual—even if it is as little as a cup of cold water (Matthew 10:42).

After Jesus taught His disciples about Him being the vine, He closed with this comment: "These things I have spoken to you so that My joy may be in you, and that your joy may be made full" (John 15:11). Jesus went to the cross facing the future with joy (Hebrews 12:2). When we move out of ourselves and let Jesus in, we are filled with His joy. Then, when we face the great challenges of life, we come to realize that the joy of the Lord is our strength (Nehemiah 8:10) and that in His presence is fullness of joy" (Psalm 16:11)!

When we are abiding in the vine, we experience God in the present tense. There is never a second when He is not actively loving us. Just as Jesus dwelt in the Father's love, so we are to constantly remind ourselves that we are being loved right at this moment. Jesus said, "Just as the Father has loved Me, I have also loved you; abide in My love" (John 15:9). We are united with the Son and the Father in love—what a staggering thought! We are transformed by revelation, not just information. When we look to ourselves, we are turning our heads away from Him. But when we turn back to Him, we realize He is the one who supplies all of our needs (Philippians 4:19).

Earlier in my experience, I thought that my needs were only physical. I have come to realize that God supplies my emotional needs as well. One experience will illustrate.

One day, I was very concerned about a circumstance close to my heart. People were hurting. There was much confusion. I approached my husband, who was enjoying sunshine on the balcony.

"I'm really worried about..." I said.

His response was, "Oh well, nothing we can do."

I felt completely alone. I decided to run away, just for a day. I decided to go to a local hotel to be by myself. I informed my husband of my decision and where he could find me in case of emergency. I gathered some clothes, snacks, and my Bible and left.

After I had checked into the hotel, I had it out with God. I questioned Him about my marriage, my family, and my life's purpose. I wrote my questions down in a notebook.

God just allowed me to rant. When I was finally exhausted, He spoke to my heart with His own questions: "Why have you made your husband God?"

I hadn't realized I had.

"You have made him responsible for all your needs, in this case, your emotional needs. That's My job," He informed me. "Didn't I tell you that I will meet all your needs? Your husband can't love you as much as I do. He doesn't know what you're thinking this moment. He hasn't counted every hair on your head, and his thoughts toward you do not outnumber the sand. It's unfair to expect that kind of intimacy from him. Further, your desire to fix everyone in your family and solve their problems is misplaced. That is not your job either. I have given you friends and family. They are gifts to you and are unlike you. Stop trying to make them a carbon copy of you."

"What am I supposed to do then?" I asked Him.

"You can start by absorbing My unfailing love for you."

After visiting with God for quite a while and then waving the white flag of surrender to His will, I slept like a baby.

Chapter 5

The Branches

We are connected to the Vine, not each other.

It's tempting to focus on the testimonies of others, all the while missing what God is doing in us personally. The purpose of our relationships with other branches is that we are to encourage each other. It's part of the fruit that God brings forth from each individual branch. The existence of the other branches also reminds us to celebrate our differences. We must caution ourselves, though, against looking for the approval of the other branches, as opposed to seeking God's approval.

A question we can ask ourselves is: "Would I do my best if there was no one around to impress?" God's direction is to do whatever we do from our hearts and for the Lord, knowing that He is the one who will reward us for our service (Colossians 3:17,23-24). God sees the heart while human beings see only the outward appearance (1 Samuel 16:7). This reminds me of the amaryllis plant that has become popular during the Christmas season. Its bulb is large and rather ugly on the outside, but, with the addition of water and time, it produces stunningly beautiful blooms.

When Jesus healed two blind men asking for a miracle, He said, "It shall be done to you according to your faith" (Matthew 9:29). According to *your* faith, not someone else's.

It's incredibly tempting for us to expect thankfulness from others when we've done things for them. I wonder how God feels when He receives so little gratitude after showering us with a multitude of blessings every day. When we do things for God in His strength, the focus changes. When we know He is pleased, we won't worry about what others think.

Scripture warns us: "The fear of man brings a snare, but he who trusts in the Lord will be exalted" (Proverbs 29:25). God is saying that worrying about the opinion the other branches have of us is dangerous. Snares don't kill at first, but they paralyze. When we focus on others, we turn away from what God is communicating to us personally. God asks us a question in Isaiah 51:12-13: "I, even I, am He who comforts you. Who are you that you are afraid of man who dies…that you have forgotten the Lord your Maker, who stretched out the heavens and laid the foundations of the earth?" How can we believe in God's love for us when we are only focused on receiving praise from one another?

Sometimes we struggle with things we don't understand. But I remember one morning when God clarified my understanding about why I was going through some of the things I was going through. Jesus said in John 15:2 that God prunes every branch that bears fruit, so that it will bear more fruit. If I am a fruitful branch, I shouldn't be surprised that some pruning will be necessary. As Jesus reminded us, it is the healthy branches that need pruning; the unfruitful branches are cut off and thrown away. God also reminded me that I would experience the fruit of righteousness as a result of the pruning, that the blessings of His love would always follow.

The apostle Paul said, "To live is Christ" (Philippians 1:21). Jesus stated that He could do nothing apart from the Father (John 5:19,30) and that we can do nothing apart from Him (John 15:5). His presence within us demonstrates His goodness to us. We must look inside and see it. Remember that "Man looks at the outward appearance, but the Lord looks at the heart" (1 Samuel 16:7).

Chapter 6

Circumstances

Regarding my circumstances, Proverbs 3:5-6 has been—and still is—a truth that helps me keep on track.

"Trust in the Lord with all your heart."

I need to ask myself: "Am I trusting? Whom do I trust—others, myself, or God? How much of my heart is involved—all of it or just some of it, depending on my feelings at the moment?"

"Do not lean on your own understanding."

The second element of this guidance is both frustrating and comforting. We're frustrated because so much of the time our circumstances just don't make sense. We are programmed to ask the questions why, how, when, and where. But, as Isaiah 55:8 reminds us, God's ways are not our ways. They are so much higher than our ways that trying to figure things out is useless. God reminds us that His plans are always better than ours, so the "B" in what we think of as "Plan B" could stand for "Best." Many times, I've had what could be described as spiritual temper tantrums, only to discover that God had a better plan. His ways are higher than ours and His thoughts higher than ours, so we must stop trying to figure out the God of the universe.

"In all your ways acknowledge Him."

Do we acknowledge Him in all our ways? Who do we give credit to when we're heading out the door and a thought pops into our head reminding us of something important that we have forgotten to do or to bring with us? Do we give ourselves credit for that perfect thought at that perfect time? Who gets the credit when we have an inspiring, creative thought?

Have you ever been searching for something and discovered that it was right before your eyes? Have you ever come across a parking spot just for you?

Just yesterday, our breakfast at a local restaurant was anonymously paid for by someone else.

A few months ago, our flat tire happened right at a coffee shop—we were able to thank the good Samaritan who helped us, not only verbally but also by supplying him with a hot coffee. Who inspired these acts of kindness? Did we remember to say thank you?

Recently, my husband forgot that he'd put his wallet on the roof of the car, only to discover that it was missing when he arrived at his destination. He returned home and searched our street to no avail. To complicate his search, there was a large delivery truck backing slowly up the street. It stopped in front of our driveway, and a burly gentleman hollered out the window to me: "Did anyone from this address lose a wallet?" And there was the answer to our panic. This man had spied the wallet on the street, checked the address from the info in it, and driven to our place to give it to us. None of the cards and money inside were missing. What are the chances of all of this happening?

Have you ever felt down and then received an encouraging call or message out of the blue? Have you ever had an inspired idea? Who gets the credit for these things happening?

A few days ago, we were searching for a new pair of black pants for my husband because of an upcoming formal occasion. We stopped into a sports store, which should have been an unlikely place to find dress pants. There was one pair, in the perfect size, that, when scanned, cost $4.00—a surprise to both the cashier and ourselves. The pants needed to be shortened, which we were told would cost $6.99. But when the call came to pick up the pants, there was no charge.

On the same day, I was searching for a velvet jacket. After no success at five stores, I decided to give it one more go. To my surprise, at the entrance of that sixth store, I met a dear friend. We decided to go for coffee. I took a quick glance around the ladies department, and there before my eyes was the jacket almost waving at me. The friend and the jacket at that exact time…what are the odds?

One day, we were having an ice cream snack and fell into conversation with another gentleman. He was visiting from out of town and just happened to be looking for the very store we were planning to visit next. What are the chances? These are small things in the big picture, but surely

God must be pleased when we acknowledge the many ways He shows His love to us.

It's so easy to take God's care of us for granted—the warmth of a home in a blizzard, air conditioning in the heat of summer, a bed to sleep on, a cat that purrs, people who make us laugh. God's love for us is as deep as the ocean and as high as the heavens. We hear stories about close calls and changed directions that have protected those involved from catastrophe. We easily see those as God's loving interventions, but what about the infinitesimal care, the tiny acts of love, He showers on us daily?

Recently, I celebrated a special birthday. I do not like to be the center of attention, and my friends were aware of that. However, one of them decided to throw a surprise party for me. I was a bit miffed at first, but she had invited a group of my closest friends, and when I settled down and chatted with God about all of this, He reminded me that this was His plan and a gift to me. I realized that much can happen in a year. My angst dissolved, and I found great reason to hug my well-wishers dearly. They are valued beyond words! Later, while visiting with the hostess of the party, she informed me that she had received the idea from God while she was vacationing in Hawaii. I'm so grateful that she followed His direction!

"And He will make your paths straight."

Other Bible versions translate this phrase as "And He will direct your paths."

That brings us back to how much we trust God's love and care for us. No matter how much I am loved by another person, that person will never know my present thoughts every moment of the day. Of course, if that person could, he or she would be God, and He sees to it that I don't place other people in His position.

When I have been lonely, He has reminded me that He will never leave me or forsake me.

When I have been fearful of the future, He has reminded me to stop worrying about tomorrow, since I don't know if I will even have another tomorrow here on earth.

When I have felt weak, He has reminded me that He is my strength.

At other times, He has invited me to come to Him, stop "doing" anything, and rest. Often, this happens when I haven't been listening to His voice and have gone running off to pursue my own agenda, accomplishing nothing of any value.

God will give us strength for His work, not our own work, so that we *can* be led forth in peace and joy (Isaiah 55:11-12).

Because God has promised to guide His children, I don't have to rush—a bad habit I've had but am learning to trust Him with. I can't imagine Jesus rushing to and fro in a frenzy to get things done. God supplies us with time to do His will.

When we acknowledge God in all our ways, we will be able to see His love all around us, because He *is* love. When we trust and don't try to figure things out ourselves, when we acknowledge that He is in control, then the promise follows that He will direct our paths. That's what a shepherd does, isn't it?

Chapter 7

Tribulation

Jesus said in John 16:33: "These things I have spoken to you so that in Me you may have peace. In the world you have tribulation, but take courage; I have overcome the world."

When I first encountered it, I really didn't like this verse. I would rather that Jesus had said that if I followed Him, I would have *no* tribulation. (There I was, leaning on

my own understanding yet again.)
However, He has taught me that His
truths are realized though experiences.
The following are experiences that
have led me to realize that He alone is
the solution.

Financial Needs

Like most people, we've had our
challenges with money.

Earlier, when we were just
beginning to learn His ways, we were
encouraged to tithe. Why, we asked.
Why does God demand that we give at
least 10 per cent of our earnings to
Him? That seemed like legalism to us.
God already owns everything, so why
would we have to give to Him?

However, relinquishing "our own
understanding," we decided to tithe
anyway. We've been amazed that God
has met our financial needs in so many
wonderful and surprising ways. Those

ways are too variable and plentiful for me to go into full detail. However, I can give some examples.

One time, we needed money to visit Australia for our son's wedding. A family member who had been saving money suddenly realized that it was for "for such a time as this" (Esther 4:14) and supplied our need.

Another time, we were down to our last $20 and decided to put it into a collection plate one Sunday morning. We did not know then that a few minutes later we would open a Christmas card containing $200 from an anonymous sender. To this day, we have never learned who the sender was, and there was no way that that person could have known that we would have "tithed" our last $20 a few minutes before receiving the card. As I said in an earlier chapter, we continue to receive God's supply, which is not just enough to meet our needs but very abundant.

We realize now that tithing is a spiritual law that includes the promise that we will reap what we sow. God is not a dictator, but our Father, who is continually showing us that His ways are not ours and that He loves us. How would we have known His care for us without having received the challenge to tithe?

Health Challenges

All of us have had health challenges. God says He is the healer, but how do we know? In our case, it's been proven through bouts of flu, colds, migraines, and broken limbs, to name just a few of the ailments we've faced. In all of these cases, we were brought to the end of ourselves, and God proved Who He is.

Danger

We continually need God's physical protection.

One morning, I was planning a trip along the freeway to an appointment about an hour away. I had read earlier that God guards our going out and our coming in (Psalm 121:8) and that He goes before us and makes the rough paces smooth (Isaiah 45:2). I headed out, happily thanking Him for those promises. There were three traffic lanes. I chose the middle one as I'd discovered that it was the most direct. To my right, I noticed a large semi-truck with signals indicating it would make a right turn at the next intersection. I was overtaking it when I noticed that it was instead moving into my lane. My automobile was in the driver's blind spot. Because there was another vehicle on my left, I couldn't escape. I hit the horn, and the other driver slowed enough for me to get past him. We both stayed in our previous lanes for another thirty minutes. Without God's "heads up" and the horn, it would have been catastrophic. God showed me His protection through experience.

Confusion

We frequently find ourselves in a state of confusion. At those times, it's wise to remember God's promises:

• "I will instruct you and teach you in the way which you should go; I will counsel you with My eye upon you" (Psalm 32:8).

• "I will even make a roadway in the wilderness, rivers in the desert" (Isaiah 43:19).

• "Christ Jesus is He who died, yes, rather who was raised, who is at the right hand of God, who also intercedes for us" (Romans 8:34).

We were staying at a hotel before moving into our new home. Our household belongings were in storage on a truck. It was the middle of January, dark and cold. My mind was assaulted by fear. Questions surfaced. Would our things fit into the smaller place? Would the renovations be completed in time? Had we made the right decision in selling our lovely home and moving into the smaller townhome? I have a baby grand piano that had fit quite nicely in our previous house, but would it fit in the new space, which would be much smaller? We had visits at the hotel from our friends, who prayed for us and encouraged us. None of them, however, could know my inward fears and thoughts. I was seeking God, losing sleep, and feeling that I wasn't getting through when the thought came: Jesus is interceding for you.

Although our friends had prayed for us, none of them could have known my inward fears in the night—but Jesus knew. That realization brought waves of relief and some tears. Of course, He knew how to pray for me. I was safe, and He was taking care of everything—and He did.

Discouragement

Discouragement often comes to plague us. Sometimes the discouragement comes from our own failures. I've fallen into the trap of looking for formulas to make my life and my relationship with God easy. The formula always fails, and I'm left puzzled and frustrated.

We have made it a habit to read scripture early in the morning before we start the day. Often God surfaces a truth or direction that gives us confidence for the day. Quite frequently, my husband and I will read different passages in the Bible and find that the message is the same in both of them. That always surprises us. I've learned that God will not be confined to a formula. He might lead us to the adventure for the day, but He doesn't want us to leave Him behind. He will go with us and direct our steps.

Sometimes, however, the pages of the Bible stay blank. At those times, I've learned that God is telling me to look back to what He has already taught me and not be looking for something fresh.

Recognizing that God is never the source of discouragement has been very freeing. When discouragement accompanies a circumstance or we experience inner darkness, we can be sure it's not of God. The circumstance might not change, but when we accept the fact that God is teaching us through that circumstance, then it becomes a wonderful opportunity to learn an important and valuable truth from Him. And again, that truth will set us free.

Isaiah 26:3 affirms: "The steadfast of mind You will keep in perfect peace, because he trusts in You."

Fatigue

Fatigue often grinds us to a halt. The answer, of course, is rest. Think of the Shepherd and His sheep. Does He badger and drive the sheep to exhaustion? No, instead the Shepherd takes His sheep to a place of rest beside still waters (Psalm 23:1-2). God further advised us in Psalm 46:10: "Cease striving and know that I am God; I will be exalted among the nations, I will be exalted in the earth." And Jesus promised in Matthew

11:28: "Come to Me all who are weary and heavy-laden, and I will give you rest."

Weakness and Oppression

There's a difference between fatigue and weakness. Weakness often comes with a sense of heaviness and oppression. This also doesn't come from God. Often the sense of weakness comes after we have sensed that God is guiding us to do something. A friend shared with me recently that she felt God had given her a message telling her to take dinner to her young family, who were struggling with some health challenges. As soon as she decided to go ahead, it seemed as if "all hell" broke loose. Frustration, concern about the meal, and a sense of weakness enveloped her. As it turned out, the meal fell together with little effort, using ingredients that were already on hand. Blessings followed for her family and herself.

If we have heard God's voice, then we must be strong and take courage. Sometimes we might have to wait for His eagle wings to carry us higher, but that, too, will come.

God doesn't tell us to submit to weakness. Repeatedly, He tells us to "Be strong and let your heart take courage" (Psalm 27:14, 31:24). We will be free from oppression when we say with the psalmist: "We will not fear" (Psalm 46:2).

The Need for Comfort

God is never the author of fear. We fear because we don't trust His love and care for us, and we can only be strong when we know we are safe. Most times, comfort comes from believing what God declares over us:

- "Do not fear, for I am with you" (Genesis 26:24).
- "I will never desert you, nor will I ever forsake you" (Hebrews 13:5).
- "Perfect love casts out fear" (1 John 4:18).
- "Say to those with anxious heart, 'Take courage, fear not. Behold, your God will come with vengeance; the recompense of God will come, but He will save you'" (Isaiah 35:4).
- "I, even I, am He who comforts you. Who are you that you are afraid of man who dies and of the son of man who is made like grass?" (Isaiah 51:12).
- "Blessed be the God and Father of our Lord Jesus Christ, the Father of mercies and God of all comfort" (2 Corinthians 1:3).
- "You are my hiding place; You preserve me from trouble; You surround me with songs of deliverance" (Psalm 32:7).

• "For God has not given us a spirit of timidity but of power and love and discipline" (2 Timothy 1:7).

Rejection

We *will* be rejected. Jesus experienced rejection, especially in his hometown and with those who had known Him since childhood. He wasn't fazed though. He continues to be rejected to this day, and so will we be. When we expect it, we won't be undone by it either.

Chapter 8

I Changed My Mind

Colossians 3:2-5 says: "Set your mind on the things above, not on the things that are on earth. For you have died and your life is hidden with Christ in God. When Christ, who is our life, is revealed, then you also will be revealed with Him in glory. Therefore consider the members of your earthly body as dead to immorality, impurity, passion, evil desire, and greed, which amounts to idolatry."

Romans 12:2 says something similar: "Be transformed by the renewing of your mind."

We often use the expression, "I changed my mind." Now science has made the "major discovery" that how we think actually has the power to change our brain chemistry. This insight, of course, is not new. Centuries ago, Proverbs 23:7 said this about human beings: "As he thinks within himself, so he is." It's just one more truth that's been rediscovered.

How do we perceive ourselves? Remember the amaryllis bulb that is large and ugly but produces a plant with stunningly beautiful blooms. What we see when we look inside ourselves, our invisible inward attitude, is more powerful than what we see in a mirror. Do we see ourselves as weak victims or as strong conquerors, as lions or as prey? We have the power to change our minds about ourselves.

What we hear also has great power to control our lives. The power of words can be used both positively (when they are God's words) or negatively (when they come from another source). Bullying has become a serious, present day problem for young people. Sometimes bullying comes out of my own mouth, directed at myself! How often have we told ourselves: "You're an idiot. That was stupid. You're old and useless. Face reality—you're weak. You'll never overcome this." The circumstances are the circumstances, but it is our fear about them that is paralyzing. Often we spend far too much time dwelling on our own frailty and the perceived judgments that others might make about us. We've all experienced this. It's accusation and condemnation, and it does *not* come from God. Judgmental attacks, doubts, and accusations didn't affect Jesus, and they don't have to affect us either.

Psalm 34:13 gives us good counsel: "Keep your tongue from evil and your lips from speaking deceit." Proverbs 18:21 says, "Death and life are in the power of the tongue." Fear based in a focus on ourselves and what others might say about us is a deception. Romans 8:6 says: "The mind set on the flesh is death, but the mind set on the Spirit is life and peace."

We must recognize the dark source of these negative judgments and stop joining "the accuser"! The fact is that we have a new, beautiful nature. Jesus died to give it to us, so let's accept it.

We can change our minds about people and pray for them instead of criticizing them. We can change our minds about life in general. If our view of life is dark and oppressive, then that view is not of God. We can starve out negative thoughts by refusing to feed them, by refusing to dwell on them and believe them.

Changing our attitude is like placing a new battery in a car. From the outside, nothing looks different. But the difference is in the power within. The car depends on the battery just as the branch depends on the vine. Neither one is the source of its own power. Jesus repeatedly tells us to "abide" in the vine (John 15:1-11). That means to just stay there, trusting in God's love, power, and provision. Our relationship to God should be as easy and comfortable as the relationship of a child who goes to his dad to ask him to fix a toy. There is no groveling, just expectation of needs being met. Sometimes a child will ask his dad to hold his hand or to carry him or to rescue him. God promises us that He will cover all of our needs.

God's mental health verse, Philippians 4:8, gives us a list of things to think about: "Whatever is true, whatever is honorable, whatever is right, whatever is pure, whatever is lovely, whatever is of good repute, if there is any excellence and if anything worthy of praise, dwell on these things." It takes intentional thinking to sieve out the good things from all of the negative thoughts that bombard us from the world around us. We are urged to take care of our physical selves through countless programs, exercises, diets, and formulas (which change constantly and are especially promoted after we have overindulged at certain seasons of the year). But do we care enough about ourselves to give the same attention to protecting and feeding our minds? Do we look inside ourselves and see sin and darkness, or do we agree with God and see the new heart He has placed within us? In Ezekiel 36:26, God promised, "I will give you a new heart and put a new spirit within you." Do we believe it, or do we doubt what God has told us? Do we look inside to see what needs to be fixed, or do we look inside and see what has already been fixed? In looking at ourselves, we must start from a place of victory, not a place of struggle.

"God is light, and in Him there is no darkness at all" (1 John 1:5). Darkness is all around us in this world. We are enticed to view a highly rated movie, only to discover that it is laced with blasphemy and vulgarity. The outside package might look beautiful and exciting, but, upon opening it, we discover the inside is negative, ugly, and dark. "Well, that's the real world," we are told, but I can go shopping or go for a walk and meet many strangers who do not pepper their conversations with vulgarity and cursing. Most people do not resort to profanity, whether they're educated or not. I'm always puzzled when Jesus' name is profaned by people who don't know Him and don't believe in Him. It makes no sense. Is it just filler to cover up their ignorance of a proper and meaningful vocabulary?

When things got rough for Jesus, we learn that He went away by Himself, sometimes to a garden or a mountaintop. That's where the mental and spiritual battles were won. We also need to go away and meditate on God's truths about ourselves. As long as the mind is enslaved, the body will never be free. Using God's Word is the ideal way to "be transformed by the renewing of your mind."

Our path in this life is to be beautiful. This is not achieved by following a formula but by having a change of mind. If I sin, it's not my nature. I choose whether to sin or not.

Because I have chosen to be connected in a relationship with Jesus, I am being transformed by the renewing of my mind—but that takes time. The apostle Paul said in Philippians 1:6: "For I am confident of this very thing, that He who began a good work in you will perfect it." Apples don't just pop onto the branch. They begin with a blossom and slowly develop to maturity. Each stage is perfect, even if not yet complete.

CHAPTER 9

NO FAIL RECIPES

Isn't it great when we find a "no fail" recipe, one that will produce a perfect meal or dessert every time?

God has a few to offer us, including: "'Though the mountains be shaken and the hills be removed, yet my unfailing love for you will not be shaken or my covenant of peace be removed,' says the Lord, who has compassion on you" (Isaiah 54:10 NIV).

God's words of love never fail: "My word…which goes forth from My mouth…will not return to Me empty, without accomplishing what I desire, and without succeeding in the matter for which I sent it" (Isaiah 55:11). God's words of love cast out fear (1 John 4:18). They're new every morning (Lamentations 3:22-23). God's love for us was demonstrated most clearly at the cross, when God declared His love for the whole world and died to prove it. Jesus' purpose for coming was to show us the extent of that love: "He who has seen Me has seen the Father" (John 14:9) and "Greater love has no one than this, that one lay down his life for his friends" (John 15:13). It was the ultimate act of love.

We've all heard these truths, but how does God's love work out in our daily lives? Scripture gives us many examples. Here are three.

1. When Jesus was being crucified, He prayed for His murderers, "Father, forgive them; for they do not know what they are doing" (Luke 23:34). I wonder if He still prays the same for us when we do things without realizing the hurt that is being caused to others. We can be awful or beautiful at any given moment, but His love for us is continual. He tells us to be like Him, to overcome evil with good and to pray for our enemies. Do we forgive those who hurt us, acknowledging that they do not know what they are doing?

2. The story of the prodigal son (Luke 15:11-32) shows us that we can run away from God and He'll watch us go and let us. His love will always

grant us that freedom. Even though the prodigal's father must have been grieved watching his son leave, he set him free and didn't go chasing him. He kept watching, though, and one day he saw his son on the horizon. He couldn't help himself and ran to meet him. There was no condemnation, just love and relief. Likewise, God loves us even when we hurt Him.

3. The story of the woman caught in adultery (John 8:1-11) is a picture of compassion, as Jesus did not throw condemning verbal stones at her. Her accusers had, but Jesus quietly told her to sin no more. Why? Because she was choosing a life far too shallow for her best, and God knew it.

And what about us, we wonder. Our relationship with God is as personal as that of the prodigal and the adulteress, and God will demonstrate His love for us in countless ways. As branches, we may have varied spiritual gifts, but without love we are like clanging cymbals (1 Corinthians 13:1).

One day shortly before Christmas, I was in a bad mood while contemplating the commercialism of the holiday. I didn't like the whole frenzy, the wide-eyed, bewildered shoppers, and the nonstop ads reminding us that the more expensive the gift, the more love. "Hurry, before it's too late!" seemed to be the message of the day. I was definitely in the minority with my attitude, but I was still dutifully shopping. I needed an attitude adjustment desperately, so I asked God to help me. (I interrupt this story to call to mind Jesus' instruction for us to *ask*—Matthew 7:7-11.)

One of the gifts I was searching for was out of stock in our town, so I had to travel half an hour to the next nearest town. It was a beautiful, sunny morning when I headed out. We live in an area surrounded by mountains, and as I drove, my eyes fell on them. The closest ones were purple, but there was a second range behind them highlighted in gold by the sun. In front of the mountains were florescent green pastures dotted with white whistler swans. Overhead, there was a V of Canada geese. I was listening to a Christmas carol when a huge crescendo climaxed with: "Oh come let us adore Him, Christ the Lord!" The thought entered my mind that Jesus had created everything that I was experiencing—the mountains, the fields, the birds, the sunshine, music. He had given me eyes to see His beauty and ears to hear His praise, as well as gas in my car and clear roads. There were just the two of us there in the car, Him and me. I realized again that Christmas was a day to celebrate Him. Suddenly, there was a lump in my throat, and there were tears in my eyes. Needless to say, God had answered my prayer for a better attitude. The true reality of Christmas is experiencing and celebrating God's unfathomable, creative, unspeakable love, and that was what I was experiencing at that moment. Information is good, but revelation is His personal touch. I had asked, and He had answered.

We should always be expecting something good, because the good and positive in any situation is where He is. We are His children, but our love for Him can't compare to His love for us. He is as real as the air, the sun, and the law of gravity. He is never not watching us. He sees His Son in me.

Do I? We must be careful to not insult His love for us.

The wondrous thing is that He fills us with His love. If we're not receiving it and soaking in it, then we can't give it away because we can only give what we have. Jesus told us to *abide* in His love.

The gift of peace can't be underestimated. He has given us His covenant of peace: "These things I have spoken to you, so that in Me you may have peace. In the world you have tribulation, but take courage; I have overcome the world" (John 16:33) and "Peace I leave with you; My peace I give to you; not as the world gives do I give to you. Do not let your heart be troubled, nor let it be fearful" (John 14:27). It's the peace that "surpasses all comprehension" (Philippians 4:7) and the "perfect peace" that comes when we keep our minds firmly fixed on Him (Isaiah 26:3), not just glancing in His direction now and then.

Jesus offers us His peace, but it must be absorbed. It should not be like a delivered package left sitting on our doorstep as the snow piles up on it and the rain wilts the packaging. Often God's peace is not recognized as the treasure it is. At other times, it is mentally accepted and brought into the house, where it is only admired from a distance and remains useless.

We need to take and use what Jesus died for.

Chapter 10

Hope

Philippians 1:6 promises us: "He who began a good work in you will perfect it."

One time, I felt very alone in my beliefs. I had discovered that other Christians had different opinions and different experiences than I did. I began to think that I was too narrow and too critical. God used Philippians 1:6 to teach me that I was indeed different from others and that He was working in me "both to will and to work for His good pleasure" (Philippians 2:13). "Well, what about everyone else?" I asked Him. "I'm working in them also," He counseled. Each one of us believers has the connection to the Vine, but it is very personal. The one thing that we have in common is His presence within. We will all bear fruit, but it will be different fruit.

What a comfort this promise is! It reminds us that God is changing us all the time. As we listen and learn, we are transformed through the truth that sets us free (John 8:32). As branches of the Vine, we learn to absorb His great love for us, and therefore we cannot help but be transformed. We learn that God calls us His children and heirs (Romans 8:16-17). He also states in

Galatians 1:16 that He is pleased to reveal His Son in us. Let that sink in.

Jesus reminds us not to worry about tomorrow (Matthew 6:34) and not to focus on our own growth (Philippians 2:4). The voice of condemnation hunkers over us, hoping to discourage us, demanding, "Are you there yet? Have you arrived? Is God pleased with you yet?"

No. Life is a journey. We are not there yet. But we are right where we are supposed to be at this moment. There are no partial births. God has taught us that there is no friendship between light and darkness (2 Corinthians 6:14, Ephesians 5:8, Colossians 1:13, 1 Thessalonians 5:5). We do not have the old sin nature. We have a new nature. There's no such thing as being "kind of born," either in the natural sphere or in the supernatural sphere. Jesus clearly said we needed to be born again, not just made a little better. Our growth, of course, is God's work, and He knows what He is doing. When we accept the Word and His promises, we become partakers of His divine nature, extensions of the Vine Himself. The branches of a vine don't worry, do they? So, why should we? How much of the Vine is not mine?

Children who take a tumble while learning to walk are not condemned and considered failures, are they? Most often, they are helped to their feet by compassionate parents or bystanders. We are to do the same thing spiritually for those in our spiritual family who take a tumble or are just learning to walk.

Sheep don't concern themselves with directing their own paths, do they? They listen and follow because they know the shepherd's voice. When

Mary Magdalene visited the empty tomb, she met someone whom she presumed was the gardener—until He spoke her name: "Mary." She recognized Jesus immediately because of His voice (John 20:11-15). A while later, two of Jesus' disciples were walking to Emmaus and discussing the latest happenings in Jerusalem. Jesus joined them, but they didn't recognize Him until, while sharing a meal with them, He broke bread, blessed it, and gave it to them. Suddenly, they recognized Him, but He vanished from their sight. They recalled how He had taught them about Himself from the scriptures (Luke 24:13-32).

Likewise today, Jesus' followers hear His voice clearly. The Bible is Jesus' voice, and His followers will hear Him speaking through it. It is vital that we practice listening. When we give ear to His voice through scripture, we will recognize Him. His message will always be bathed in love.

If there was a huge crowd and the voice of one of my children called out, I would recognize it. God does the same. He will hear our voices above the crowd when we call to Him. We should always expect His love to show up, minute by minute. Remember that God is now. He describes Himself as "I am." Like the air we are breathing and the gravity holding us on this planet, He is unchangeable. He is the same yesterday, today, and forever (Hebrews 13:8). He goes before us and makes the rough places smooth (Isaiah 45:2). The path of the righteous grows brighter and brighter until the full day (Proverbs 4:18). And even to our old age He is the same (Isaiah 46:4).

Chapter 11

Deception

Deception is a reality, and it is frequently described as freedom. The author of deception is pleased when we get sidetracked. Often the deceiver's voice uses fine-sounding, "logical" arguments. In my case, before I met Jesus, deception was the driving force in my life. I was encouraged to dwell on myself, check off all the great things I had accomplished and bask in how wonderful I was. Education was right up there as something to strive for and as a sure pathway to fame. Material possessions came a close second and could easily become an object of worship. Family, home, and status were also desired. All of these goals were, and are, great, but they were never completely satisfying.

In John 8:44, Jesus described the devil as "a liar and the father of lies." Jesus further explained in John 10:10: "The thief comes only to steal and kill, and destroy; I came that they may have life, and have it abundantly." So, what does this abundant life that Jesus spoke of mean? I came to realize that lofty goals and material possessions can all disappear. Family, status, home, and health can come crashing down, and all the education in the world will never heal a broken heart. I came to realize the abundant life Jesus was speaking of was His own. As I thought about Jesus walking this earth, I observed that He demonstrated wisdom, security, peace, gentleness, kindness, love, compassion, and confidence, all while not getting caught up in the frenzy.

Before His public ministry, Jesus was led into the desert to straighten things out with the deceiver (Matthew 4:1-11). The first temptation was an attack on His identity: "If You are the Son of God, command that these stones become bread." Jesus replied that man does not live on bread alone but on every word that proceeds out of the mouth of God. The deceiver then tried to make Jesus do something foolish (jump off a tower) to draw attention to Himself and increase His fame. That didn't work, so he then offered Jesus the wealth of the world, in exchange for worship. That failed as well.

We are offered the same temptations in a myriad of different ways. As Christians, the voice of the deceiver constantly tries to cause us to doubt our identity. At the slightest stumble, the voice charges in, accusing us of failure. When we are successful and see fruit in our lives, the voice quickly accuses us of pride. The solution to all of this is to do what Jesus did and fight back with God's Word: "Therefore there is now no condemnation for those who are in Christ Jesus" (Romans 8:1). As well, I know I can do nothing of myself, but any good I do comes from Jesus living within me (John 5:19,30, 7:26, 8:28, 9:33, 15:5, Romans 7:18, 1 Corinthians 9:16). It's His power!

There is a very real deception that constantly plays out in the culture around us. It goes like this: "We should all embrace our own beliefs. There's one God for us all. It doesn't matter what you believe. We can all do what we want." The problem surfaces when doing what we want causes suffering for others. Murder, stealing, and lying have a source, and that source is not God. We don't have to look far to see darkness in this world. Many will say that they are born that way. I agree. We're all born very much imperfect, with a proud, rebellious nature. Is it any wonder that Jesus said we needed to be born again?

Jesus declared: "I am the light of the world; he who follows Me will not walk in the darkness, but will have the Light of life" (John 8:12). The greatest deception of all is to keep humanity in the dark about the deceiver's very existence. "Anyone but Jesus" seems to be the prevailing attitude of many.

We must ask ourselves where that thought comes from, when Jesus has promised life abundant.

We must be careful that we don't throw stones at the deceived. Jesus never did. He offered revelation and compassion. We are to do the same. The woman caught in adultery, the blind man, the lepers, the thief crucified with Him—all who met Jesus were offered love and compassion. Jesus proclaimed: "I, if I am lifted up from the earth [that is, on the cross], will draw all men to Myself" (John 12:32). He also stated: "No one can come to Me unless the Father who sent Me draws him" (John 6:44). We're also reminded that "The Lord…is patient toward you, not wishing for any to perish but for all to come to repentance" (2 Peter 3:9).

Jesus is described as the Lion of Judah (Revelation 5:5). The deceiver is described as prowling around "*like* a roaring lion" (1 Peter 5:8).

Jesus is "the Light of the world" (John 8:12). The deceiver "disguises himself as an angel of light" (2 Corinthians 11:14).

Jesus is described as the Lamb of God (John 1:29). The deceiver is described as a wolf dressed in sheep's clothing (Matthew 7:15).

Jesus invited us to come to Him and promised that, if we did, He would give us rest (Matthew 11:28). The deceiver tells us to "keep trying!" He'll entice us to fight a battle that we'll never win because it's already been won by Jesus. When we fail, he'll be ready with more accusations.

The enemy wants us to stop acknowledging God because when we acknowledge Jesus, we'll discover love. Jesus acknowledged God as His Father and said that His love for us was the same as the Father's love for Him (John 17:23).

The enemy wants us to be fearful, to keep asking, "What will happen if…?" Have you ever noticed that this question usually leads to some form of darkness? Pictures surface in our imaginations of accidents, sickness, failure, and loneliness. Have you also noticed that most of these fears have never materialized?

This past Valentine's Day, I read Romans 8:34-39. There we are reminded that Jesus is always interceding for us and that nothing will ever separate us from His love—not "tribulation, or distress, or persecution, or famine, or nakedness, or peril, or sword…neither death, nor life, nor angels, nor principalities, nor things present, nor things to come, nor powers, nor height, nor depth, nor any other created thing." Verse 37, placed

in the middle of this passage, reads,
"But in all these things we
overwhelmingly conquer through Him
who loved us." I meditated on this for
a while and felt God clarifying its
meaning. We all experience
challenges and difficulties, and the
enemy wants us to immediately
question God's love for us. It's then
that we should recall the promises
about God's love in Romans 8:37-39.
I especially appreciated that this
message came to me on Valentine's
Day.

An earlier experience was
instructive for both my husband and
me. We had been given an opportunity
to encourage a class of young married
couples. As the lessons moved along,
we experienced darkness between us.
It was like a wall. We were to the point
of shelving the whole thing until one
morning I read Ephesians 6:12. I was

convinced that God was using that verse to clarify what was happening: "For our struggle is not against flesh and blood [that is, each other], but against the rulers, against the powers, against the world forces of darkness, against the spiritual forces of wickedness in the heavenly places." I timidly approached my husband Barry and suggested that perhaps we were being attacked by a common enemy whose goal was to have us hate each other and cancel the class. Immediately, the darkness between us dissipated, as we both realized the truth. That made us free, and that kept us going successfully until the end of the sessions.

The enemy comes to steal our joy, confidence, peace, trust, identity, protection, and unity with the Father and Jesus. But God says He "has not given us a spirit of timidity [or fear], but of power and love and discipline" (2 Timothy 1:7).

Wisdom and revelation are gifts to us from the King of the universe. 2 Thessalonians 3:3 promises, "But the Lord is faithful, and He will strengthen and protect you from the evil one." 2 Timothy 4:18 encourages us with these words: "The lord will rescue me from every evil deed, and will bring me safely to His heavenly kingdom; to Him be the glory forever and ever." Amen!

Jesus' words ring out that He has come to set us free (Luke 4:18). That freedom is in the heart. An illustration might help here. Imagine a bird in a cage. How sad, we might think. But what if the door to the cage is open? Now the bird has a choice. It can fly out to freedom into a bigger world. It can also stay in the present environment, where it might find inner freedom. The cage can be a place of peace and protection. "Man looks at the outward appearance, but the Lord looks at the heart" (1 Samuel 16:7).

Another ploy of the enemy is to keep us from reading God's Word. Why? Because the Word (Jesus) became flesh (John 1:1). He and the Word of God are one. The enemy will also use distractions when we do read the Bible—the phone will ring, or someone will send us a text, or the cat will throw up, or the thought of food will surface, and on and on.

The deceiver is real, but God's warning and promise are clear: Do not be deceived.

Chapter 12

God's Voice

God the Father invites us to be part of His family. Jesus declared: "I am the way, and the truth, and the life; no one comes to the Father but through Me" (John 14:6).

Jesus is the Word made flesh, and as we meditate on God's Word, we're actually meditating on Jesus. There is a huge difference between knowing scripture and having God's Holy Spirit bring us understanding of and insight into the meaning of the scripture. It is the difference between knowledge and revelation. Here are a few examples:

• *"Therefore there is now no condemnation for those who are in Christ Jesus" (Romans 8:1)*. If we are under condemnation, we won't have power to overcome.

• *"The steadfast of mind You will keep in perfect peace, because he trusts in You" (Isaiah 26:3)*. It is perfectly possible to keep our minds on God through His Holy Spirit's enablement.

• *"Today if you hear His voice, do not harden your hearts" (Hebrews 3:15)*. Hardened hearts can't see miracles. Soft, expectant hearts experience God's presence in a myriad of ways.

• *"If the Son makes you free, you will be free indeed" (John 8:36)*. Self-control may appear to be bondage, but in reality it is the gift of God setting us free. And it's not *our* self-control but the presence of God within. The apostle Paul said, "I can do all things through Him who strengthens me" (Philippians 4:13).

• *"The joy of the Lord is your strength" (Nehemiah 8:10).* This is the same joy that strengthened Jesus as He faced the cross (Hebrews 12:2). Joy is power.

• *"For we are His workmanship, created in Christ Jesus for good works, which God prepared beforehand so that we would walk in them" (Ephesians 2:10).* We don't head off with our list of things to do *for* God, so that He'll be pleased with our efforts at the end of the day. Rather, it's the Holy Spirit doing things through us—as Paul said, "Not I, but Christ" (Galatians 2:20 KJV). We'll recognize the good works He has planned when we find strength and joy in what we do and as we listen to His inner guidance. Unlike others, we will receive Jesus' personal, individual guidance.

• *"He has rescued us from the domain of darkness and transferred us to the kingdom of His beloved Son" (Colossians 1:13).* Note that this is past tense; it has already been accomplished. Compare God's kingdom to the world we live in, where there is evil, sadness, fear, failure, depression, and hopelessness. Looking at it from the outside, the domain of darkness seems so small compared to the things God has created. It is like comparing a human mansion with one of God's mountains.

God has placed us in a large place, which He calls His "hiding place" (Psalm 32:7, 119:114). I used to think His hiding place was very tiny. I now realize that His hiding place is mammoth. It's His kingdom. Remember the prayer Jesus taught us: "Your kingdom come. Your will be done, on earth as it is in heaven" (Matthew 6:10). God's large place is saturated with joy, peace, hope, protection, and power. We can cry in joyous response: "You, O Lord, are a shield about me; my glory, and the One who lifts my head" (Psalm 3:3).

Chapter 13

Freedom

One of Jesus' gifts to us is peace, which is the path to freedom. However, like a cool drink on a hot day, we must take the vessel in our hands, put it to our mouths, and drink. Peace is to be received, not just acknowledged as a good thing. When we take it in, we are empowered and strengthened, knowing that peace is an indication of God's love for us.

There is a progression in Jesus' teaching about freedom: "I am the way, and the truth, and the life" (John 14:6); "You will know the truth, and the truth will make you free" (John 8:32); "If the Son makes you free, you will be free indeed" (John 8:36).

Jesus also said, "I came that they may have life, and have it abundantly" (John 10:10). When we are free, we have power. 2 Corinthians 4:7 describes the power, like a great treasure, that God has placed within us: "We have this treasure in earthen vessels, so that the surpassing greatness of the power will be of God, and not from ourselves." (That is very similar to the image of a branch receiving its life from the vine.) We must accept the fact that it's His power and not ours. Looking at the treasure is wonderful, but taking it out of the box and putting it to use is what pleases the

Father. What good is a weapon or the key to a new car if we never use it?

"Man looks at the outward appearance, but the Lord looks at the heart" (1 Samuel 16:7). Therefore, we shouldn't be surprised that the packaging of the treasure might look a little weather-beaten and roughed up. Since Jesus' Word is the power that fuels the universe, taking it in like spiritual medicine will ignite power within us. Jesus told His disciples that He only spoke what his Father told Him to speak (John 8:28): "It is the Spirit who gives life…the words that I have spoken to you are spirit and are life" (John 6:63). His words declared His dependency. In the same way, we will never know the power of God until we declare our dependency on Him and decide to use the power He has given us. God declares that His Word will not return to Him empty, without accomplishing His purpose (Isaiah 55:11). He assumes responsibility for it. There is a qualification though. If we do not use words drenched in His love and compassion, then there will be no power. We will be wasting our time.

Peace is an indication of God's power. God promises: "You will go out with joy and be led forth with peace" (Isaiah 55:12). God also tells us: "Let the peace of Christ rule in your hearts" (Colossians 3:15). Even in the presence of darkness and oppression, God's peace must prevail. I have found this guidance to be true and helpful in daily experience. I can face giants if I am at peace.

One example comes to mind. We were living in an area of the country where the economy was struggling. My husband's employment changed, and he went from being a salesman to stocking warehouse shelves for the same company. It meant shift work. I was teaching piano at the time, and students were coming in throughout the day, before school, during lunch hour, and after school. This presented a sleeping challenge for my husband. Our two young adult children were completing secondary school and were flapping their wings, preparing to fly from our nest. One day while I was walking with a friend, she suggested that my husband could find work in a province about 3,000 miles away to the west, where her family was moving to shortly. Since our daughter had applied to attend school there, it was a thought that we were willing to entertain. Looking back, our decision was ridiculous, completely contrary to common sense. The job description was completely different from any work my husband had done previously. It would mean selling our home in the coldest, snowiest month of the year, in the middle of a recession. God has promised in scripture: "I will give them one heart and one way, that they may fear Me always, for their own good and for the good of their children after them." We followed God's Word, and that gave us peace, a peace which surpassed all comprehension (Philippians 4:7). There was an assurance deep in our hearts that enabled us to take the risk and follow a course that defied all logic. God's Word did not return to Him empty. The move was good for us and for our children. It sparked a sense of adventure in both of our children, which continues to this day, and as a result their lives have not become stagnant. We ended up with a lovely home and a mountain view that I could never in a million years have planned.

I could write more of our stories and fill the remainder of this book with them, but they are unique to us.

The story of the prodigal son (Luke 15:11-32) is a great illustration of humans' search for freedom "out there." He had the money, time, youthfulness, and desire to go for it, and so he did. He learned a lot during his experience, but it all culminated in the insight that what he had left was what he was looking for. The father who loved him had let him go. Love doesn't force but gives freedom. On his return home, the father ran to meet him without condemnation. What a surprise it must have been! What a relief! Not only was he greeted with acceptance and love, but a party was planned and celebrated. That's what God's grace is. Perhaps that's when the son received the new heart and the new spirit promised in Ezekiel 36:26.

Perhaps that's when he experienced being delivered "out of the pit of destruction" which God promised in Psalm 40. That pit is deception. The deceiver's voice declares in our minds that we don't need God. Satan selfishly takes. When we accept his offers, we receive fear and darkness, and we empower him. God sacrificially gives. When we accept His presence, we are empowered. Evil is a reality, but so is God. There is nothing random about life on planet earth.

When we deny what Jesus died for, we deny Him. When we deny the Word made flesh, we deny Him. We need to receive what Jesus died to give us.

When we are free, it gives glory to Jesus. Freedom is not something we have achieved but something we have accepted. We are not to fight *for* freedom, but we are to fight *from* a place of freedom. As long as the mind is enslaved to legalism, the body will never be free. Children don't try to earn their parents' protection and care—they just expect it.

"There is now no condemnation for those who are in Christ Jesus" (Romans 8:1). We are not the same people we were before we opened our lives to Him. We have been born again, with a new life and a new nature!

I have written this book to encourage readers to listen for God's voice, to stay dependent, and to be expectant. God said in Jeremiah 33:3: "Call to Me and I will answer you, and I will tell you great and mighty things, which you do not know." If we call to Him (stay dependent on Him), He *will* answer us. And the truth (Jesus Himself) will set us free. Jesus declared that He could do nothing of Himself but that He was dependent on the Father. That is an example for us, so that we will also be dependent on God—and then we will be free.

Chapter 14

The 2020 Storm

I was about to move forward to publication of this book when the COVID-19 pandemic hit. Like everyone else, I was affected. It seemed as if the whole world had been put on "pause." As I observed my friends and family members, I realized that each one was handling the storm on a personal level. Some were terrified, paralyzed by the fear of the unknown. Others were remaining in the peace that surpasses all comprehension.

Trying to understand what was going on was like wandering in a maze or in a dark hallway. Contradictory news reports still continue to bring confusion, leading to more fear. For me personally, I decided at the outset that the only thing I could control was myself. Maintaining physical health was good, but even more important was a healthy mind—and a healthy mind is one that is not dominated by fear. 2 Timothy 1:7 (NKJV) declares: "God has not given us a spirit of fear." So where does fear come from? Of course, the source is the enemy.

I decided to test myself as is taught in 2 Corinthians 13:5: "Test yourself to see if you are in the faith; examine yourselves! Or do you not recognize this about yourselves, that

Jesus Christ is in you—unless indeed you fail the test." Instead of fear, God has given us a spirit "of power and of love and of a sound mind" (2 Timothy 1:7 NKJV). As I said previously, we can only see what we are looking at. Focusing on Jesus the Vine allows my imagination to see who He is and what He is not. He is not frantic, like a deer frozen in the headlights, nor is He wringing His hands about the future. Instead, He is peace itself.

Jesus promised: "Peace I leave with you. My peace I give to you; not as the world gives do I give to you. Do not let your heart be troubled, nor let it be fearful" (John 14:27). That is where I'm staying, in the peace that Jesus gives, in the freedom of dependence on Him.